16 Duets for C Instruments - Flute and others

Two For Christmas

James Curnow

CURNOW®
MUSIC

EXCLUSIVELY DISTRIBUTED BY

HAL•LEONARD®
CORPORATION

7777 W. BLUEMOUND RD. P.O. BOX 13819 MILWAUKEE, WI 53213

Order Number: CMP 0345-00-401

James Curnow
Two For Christmas
C Instruments

ISBN 978-90-431-1037-2

Two For Christmas

Sixteen Unaccompanied Duets for Christmas
For any Instruments

Christmas Greetings!

Music at Christmas is an extremely important part of celebrating this most wonderful time of year. We hear music everywhere; on the radio, on television, in school, in church, while shopping or at Christmas get-togethers. Music adds joy and happiness and enables each of us the opportunity to join in the fun.

These easy duets are designed to allow the average to advanced players the opportunity to perform sixteen familiar carols in school, in public or anywhere Christmas is being celebrated. No accompaniment is necessary. They may be played by any combination of woodwind, brass, string or mallet percussion instruments.

Below is an instrumentation guide that tells you the appropriate book to purchase for your instrument. For example, an instrument in C may combine with an instrument in B♭, E♭, F, Bass Clef or any Mallet Percussion instrument, or a B♭ instrument may combine with instruments in C, E♭, F, Bass Clef or any Mallet Percussion instrument, etc. by purchasing the books in the appropriate key.

Most of all have fun and join in the celebration.

James Curnow
Composer/arranger

Instrumentation Guide

<u>C Instrument</u> (CMP 0345.00) - Violin, Piccolo, Flute, Oboe, or any Mallet Percussion instrument.

<u>B♭ Instrument</u> (CMP 0346.00) - B♭ Clarinet, B♭ Bass Clarinet, B♭ Cornet, B♭ Trumpet, B♭ Flugel Horn, B♭ Tenor Saxophone (play first part only), Trombone T.C., Euphonium/Baritone T.C., Tuba T.C. (play second part only).

<u>E♭ Instrument</u> (CMP 0347.00) - E♭ Alto Clarinet, E♭ Alto Saxophone, E♭ Baritone Saxophone (play second part only), E♭ Tuba T.C. (play second part only).

<u>F/E♭ Instrument</u> (CMP 0348.00) - F/E♭ Horn

<u>Bass Clef Instrument</u> (CMP 0349.00) - Cello, Double Bass (play second part only), Bassoon, Trombone B.C., Euphonium/Baritone B.C., Tuba B.C. (play second part only).

Table of Contents

TWO FOR CHRISTMAS

James Curnow (ASCAP)

1. Joy To The World

2. Coventry Carol

3. Angels We Have Heard On High

4. Good King Wenceslas

5. O Come, O Come, Immanuel

6. God Rest You, Merry Gentlemen

7. Jolly Old Saint Nicholas

8. Hark! The Herald Angels Sing

9. Polish Carol

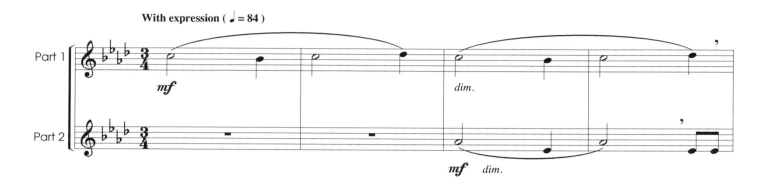

10. O Come, Little Children

11. Jingle Bells

12. Carol Of The Bells

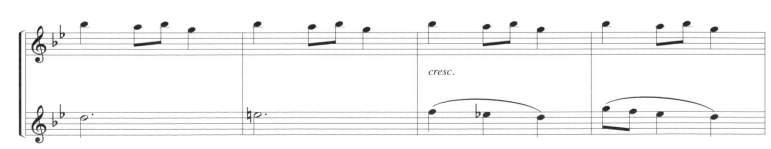

13. In The Bleak Mid-Winter

14. Deck The Halls

15. Come, All Ye Shepherds

16. We Wish You A Merry Christmas